P9-CJC-314

Understanding the Highly Sensitive Child

Seeing an Overwhelming World through Their Eyes

James Williams

© 2014 James Williams

First Published 2014 this edition 2017

All rights reserved. No part of this book may be reproduced, adapted, stored in a retrieval system or transmitted by any means, electronic, mechanical, photocopying, or otherwise without the prior written permission of the author.

The rights of James Williams to be identified as the author of this work have been asserted in accordance with the Copyright, Designs and Patents Act 1988.

A CIP catalogue record for this book is available from the British Library.

ISBN: 978-15078800-2-9

Book formatting by www.ebooksbydesign.co

Contents

Foreword by Elaine N. Aron, Ph.D.

As the author of this truly brilliant little book, James Williams explains that he is not an academic or a psychologist. I am simply a man who feels very passionately about the subject. He is highly sensitive and so is one of his daughters, and he writes about sensitivity with both simplicity and depth. His sensitivity also shows in his book's briefness. Caregivers of children need an author to get to the point so they can go get groceries, pick up the kids etc. James' book can be read in an hour, yet it has charming examples as well as great suggestions and a full, scientifically accurate description of the trait. James is reaching out to all parents, carers and teachers of sensitive children and whether through this book or on his website, he is a wonderful resource.

Elaine N. Aron, Ph.D., is the author of the worldwide bestsellers The Highly Sensitive Person and The Highly Sensitive Child, she has pioneered the research into Highly Sensitive People.

Introduction

Welcome to this little guide to understanding the highly sensitive child. The aim of this book is simple: to help you experience the world from the child's perspective, so that you can better understand them.

A little about me

I'm not an academic. I'm not a psychologist. I'm simply a man who is very, very passionate about the subject because:

- I am a highly sensitive person.

- I have a highly sensitive daughter (and a non-highly sensitive daughter).

High sensitivity has a massive impact on my family's life, and coming to understand the trait has transformed our lives – for the better. Before we understood high sensitivity we were bumbling about in the dark; now we're in the light.

I wish the entire world knew all about high sensitivity. What a wonderful world it would be if highly sensitive children and people were understood, accepted and truly valued for who they are.

All I can do is keep spreading the word, and hope that eventually everyone connected with children; teachers, health and medical professionals, care workers, parents etc. recognize without judgement, value and nurture highly sensitive children.

You can connect, keep up with our latest news, books and thinking via these channels:

- **Facebook:** www.facebook.com/MyHighlySensitiveChild

- **Twitter:** https://twitter.com/FamilyFeelings

- **Website community and blog:** http://FamilyFeelings.today/

A little about the book

The book is for anyone who is caring for or working with a highly sensitive child, from parents and grandparents to teachers and nursery staff.

The single most effective way to help a highly sensitive child is to *attune* to them, which means tuning in to their experience. To be attuned you need to watch the child carefully, and encourage them to share their thoughts and feelings. This demands a commitment of time and focus, and suspending your own judgement. It also requires you to have a good understanding of the high sensitivity trait – and that's where this book comes in.

In this simple, concise guide I distil the reams of information available on the highly sensitive child so that you can get the knowledge you need quickly and easily.

For the purposes of providing the child's perspective, in this book I use two characters:

- **Arthur** is highly sensitive across many areas. He embodies many of the traits of high sensitivity.

- **Kathryn**, Arthur's sister, isn't highly sensitive at all (she's a non-highly sensitive child).

Arthur and Kathryn do not represent real individuals, but are simplified examples. Each highly sensitive child is different, and not all are like Arthur. So in sidebars I include examples of what life is like for other highly sensitive children.

Finally, thank you to all the highly sensitive children and parents from the online community and social media channels who inspired, contributed to and supported the writing of this book. Together, I believe we're making a difference.

Chapter 1: Building Your Knowledge

Before you can think about experiencing the world from the perspective of a highly sensitive child, you need to know the answers to two basic questions:

- What is 'highly sensitive'?
- How can you tell whether a child is highly sensitive?

This first chapter aims to help you answer these questions. Then, once you understand the basics of the highly sensitive trait, you have a foundation of knowledge on which you can build in the following chapters.

How you may use this chapter depends on your current level of understanding:

- **Settled in the highly sensitive world:** You already know a good deal about the trait. Perhaps you've read Dr Elaine Aron's *The Highly Sensitive Child*, and looked at other materials online. You're ready to deepen your understanding so that you can help a highly sensitive child to grow and thrive. You may want to refresh your knowledge of the basics here before moving on; alternatively, feel free to skip this chapter and head straight to Chapter 2.

- **New to the highly sensitive world:** First and foremost, welcome! This world may seem a little strange and daunting at first, but in no time you'll be feeling at home, and benefiting hugely from ideas, strategies and support from others who are living with the trait. Chapter 1 is your starting place. And if you're caring for a child who *is* highly sensitive, the understanding you'll gain here will be life-changing.

A brief history of 'highly sensitive'

Anyone who's highly sensitive owes a debt of thanks to one lady: Elaine N. Aron. It was Dr Aron who, in the 1980s, first coined the term 'highly sensitive' in her book *The Highly Sensitive Person*. In doing so, she took highly sensitive people out of the shadow of labels like 'shy', 'introverted', 'inhibited' and 'fearful' – which do not describe us all – and for the first time introduced the notion that highly sensitive has a positive side. All of the basic information we know about highly sensitive people stems from Dr Aron's ground-breaking work, and I can't recommend her books and articles highly enough to anyone looking to understand high sensitivity. To find out more, visit her website at www.hsperson.com.

What is 'highly sensitive'?

High sensitivity is a personality trait. In this section I give you a crash course in what being highly sensitive is all about.

What does it mean to be highly sensitive?

A highly sensitive child has a very sensitive nervous system. That means they process information from the senses more deeply and more thoroughly than a non-highly sensitive child. That leads to:

1. **Keen awareness:** They notice many, many tiny details and subtleties that a non-highly sensitive child may not, and they think about these. They can't turn off this constant awareness of the world around them and of their inner world of thoughts and feelings.

2. **Intense experiencing:** They experience – *feel* – very, very intensely. It's like they have an inner intensity dial that's turned up several notches beyond the setting for a non-highly sensitive child.

3. **Overload:** All this awareness and intensity is exhausting. Like a small baby bewildered by lots of noise and movement and colourful toys, the highly sensitive child becomes overwhelmed. An overpowering need to stop the overload grows. They may rail against what's wearing them out; they may withdraw quietly into themselves; they may walk away, find a quiet space and zone out for a bit.

Chapters 2, 3 and 4 focus on these elements of the trait from the highly sensitive child's perspective.

Separating 'nice' and 'sensitive'

Imagine two parents having coffee. Jane has a highly sensitive child and knows all about the trait. Bob has a non-highly sensitive child and knows nothing of the trait. Jane is attempting to explain to Bob why her child is a little different to his. She says (bluntly!), 'My daughter is a highly sensitive child and yours isn't.' How does Bob react? I bet he bristles, because what he hears is: 'Your child is insensitive. Your child isn't as *nice* as mine.'

Jane isn't saying that at all. All she's saying is that her daughter's nervous system is much more sensitive. That's not nicer or better. It's just a bit different.

Bob's daughter isn't *in*sensitive – she's simply not *highly* sensitive: she's a non-highly sensitive child.

What's a highly sensitive child like?

No child would perfectly fit any description I could write of a highly sensitive child. Some are extraverted; some are introverted. Some cower in noisy, busy places; some seem fairly oblivious. Some get labelled 'scaredy cat'; some are little thrill-seekers. (On her website Elaine Aron has the definitive checklist of markers – see www.hsperson.com/pages/test_child.htm.)

Arthur embodies a wide range of the high sensitivity characteristics:

Arthur is generally a quiet boy. He doesn't like lots of noise and fuss. He doesn't like big changes or sudden shocks – he may jump at the slightest thing. He picks up on tiny details – Mum's changed the air freshener; Dad's belt is upside down. He doesn't love coarse textures against his skin; he needs his socks to be on perfectly straight or they bother him. When he falls and grazes his knee, it really, really hurts. When someone is mean to him, it really, really hurts. Sometimes, the world gets too much, and Arthur 'melts down' – crying, raging, climbing the walls through overstimulation.

People say of Arthur that he's 'old beyond his years' – he has an impressive vocabulary, he asks clever questions, he makes adults laugh, he likes everything just so.

He's also remarkably perceptive about what other people are thinking or feeling, and he's thoughtful: before diving in to a new situation, Arthur holds back and weighs up his options. He's at his best when people treat him with respect and guide him gently.

The child you know may be a lot like Arthur, or only a little, but if they are highly sensitive then it's likely that something in the description of Arthur will strike a chord with you.

Highly sensitive children have various needs. Fulfil these needs and they're content. Ignore these needs and they flounder. Chapter 5 looks at the needs of the highly sensitive child.

Who is highly sensitive?

Studies indicate that around one in five people (children and adults) are highly sensitive. Within high sensitivity, lots of variations exist:

- Some highly sensitive children are more sensitive than others. A child may be so sensitive that school is a real problem, for example. Or they may be just a little more sensitive than non-highly sensitive children.

- Some are sensitive in more areas than others. A child may only display extremely sensitivity in a couple of areas – they detest too much noise, for instance, and startle easily. Or they may be very sensitive in all sorts of ways.

When does a child become highly sensitive?

A child doesn't become highly sensitive, they are highly sensitive – always. The height of their sensitivity may vary over time, but they won't ever be a non-highly sensitive child.

Why are people highly sensitive?

Because they're made that way. You don't learn to be highly sensitive; you don't develop the trait because of your surroundings. A highly sensitive child has been highly sensitive since the day they were born. Which means they have no more choice over this part of who they are than, say, their height or their eye colour or the sound of their laugh.

What's up with being highly sensitive?

Absolutely nothing. That's the truth.

The highly sensitive child isn't ill or damaged in some way. You don't need to cart them off to a doctor and get a diagnosis, and then hunt for a 'cure'. High sensitivity is simply a personality trait, like being conscientious or being agreeable. It's normal to be highly sensitive.

It's *normal* to be highly sensitive. But it is *hard* to be a highly sensitive child in today's world. Because highly sensitive children are a little different. And too often people see different as 'odd' or 'wrong'.

Chapter 6 looks at what it's like to be different because of highly sensitive.

How can you tell whether a child is highly sensitive?

It's beyond the scope of this book to detail all the ways in which a child may show signs of high sensitivity. But you can find all you need with no more than an hour's reading:

1. **Find out about high sensitivity.** Read the Introduction and Chapter 1 of Elaine Aron's *The Highly Sensitive Child*. I provide a list of other good resources at http://familyfeelings.today/resources.

2. **Take Elaine Aron's Parent's Test.** You can find this in *The Highly Sensitive Child* book, or online at www.hsperson.com/pages/test_child.htm. You may tick just about every item on the checklist of highly sensitive markers to describe the child, or you may check only a couple but feel the child is strongly exhibiting those signs. Either way, if items on that checklist ring a bell for you then the child is probably highly sensitive.

Why didn't somebody *tell* me?!

As you read this chapter, you may have thought, *Why don't I already know about all this stuff? If so many people are highly sensitive, why isn't the trait common knowledge?* I don't have an answer to these questions. I wish the entire world knew all about high sensitivity. How much easier life would be for highly sensitive children if everyone understood them, and accepted them as they are. All we can do is keep spreading the word, and hope that eventually everyone connected with children – teachers, health professionals, care workers, parents – recognises, values and nurtures highly sensitive children.

Chapter 2: Noticing and Pondering

The mind of a highly sensitive child is always whirring – processing loads of details that the senses pick up on and thinking deeply. This chapter takes a look at how much highly sensitive children notice, and how much of their inner world is devoted to pondering.

Picking up on subtleties

Wherever they go and whatever they do, the highly sensitive child gathers a vast amount of information with their senses – more so than a non-highly sensitive child.

Environment

Imagine Kathryn and Arthur in a cafe with their mother:

Kathryn smells freshly brewed coffee. She sees a colourful poster on the wall. She tastes chocolate as she sips her milkshake. She feels the seat cushion, and finds the fabric soft. She hears Mum talking and, in the background, a hum of conversation and the coffee machine.

Arthur smells freshly brewed coffee, cinnamon buns, cigarette smoke, bleach, sweat and perfume. He sees a blue, orange, red and yellow poster with pictures of four different types of bird and information about the rainforest printed in two different black typefaces in varying sizes. He tastes chocolate and milk and a hint of orange as he sips his milkshake. He feels the seat cushion, and finds the fabric soft and bobbly and warm and a little itchy. He hears Mum talking, and twenty other people talking, and a baby grumbling, and a lady humming, and the coffee machine hissing, and the dishwasher whirring, and ceramic cups clinking, and, outside, a dog barking and an engine revving.

Kathryn doesn't absorb many details of the environment. Arthur does.

Moaning Max

Max can come across as a bit of a grumbler. It's winter and the central heating is on, but Max keeps moaning that he's cold and the air is too stuffy. It's summer and the family's having a lovely day out at the beach, but Max keeps complaining that he's too hot and the sand is scratchy. At a low level, sensory input is making Max uncomfortable, and he shares that fact with others in the hope of that they'll help him feel better. But usually Mum and Dad just tell Max off for being negative or silly; the environment doesn't bother them, after all.

People

Back in the cafe, let's add in the people factor:

> *As Kathryn chats away, she is aware that Mum is happy.*
>
> *Arthur notices that Mum's smile is a little fixed, her tone of voice has an edge and her eyes keep drifting to cast longing looks at the door. She's happy, he senses – but also weary.*

Arthur intuitively picks up on how people are feeling. He notices every little nuance in their tone of voice, their gestures, their facial expressions.

There's a lot going on for Arthur here. And that's before he even begins to *think* about what he's noticing...

Thinking – a lot

Remember the definition: *A highly sensitive child processes information from the senses more deeply and more thoroughly than a non-highly sensitive child.* Processing involves lots of thinking.

Clever-but-Clueless Kevin

Kevin's a really clever boy – everyone says so. He's a mine of information, and adults often comment that he converses on their level. Kevin's mum is very proud of her intelligent son. But sometimes she finds herself wondering about that intelligence! While Kevin is impressively advanced in some areas, he can be a little clueless in others. Sometimes he lacks common sense; he's so lost in Big Thoughts that he neglects to think Little Ones. He also bamboozles his mother with nonsensical talk at times as he verbalises his thought process.

Back to the cafe:

Kathryn is focusing on her chat with Mum, and right now she's thinking about – and talking about – plans for her upcoming birthday party. That's it.

Arthur, meanwhile, is thinking: What tune is that lady humming? It sounds like the one from the toothpaste commercial. What type of bird is that on the poster? And why does this cafe have a poster about rainforests? Kathryn's party – a princess cake – I don't like icing. That man is laughing very loudly – why? What's funny? Something's burning – oh look, the toasted teacake. It's all black. I wonder why burnt things go black. Kathryn's party – a soft-play centre? I was hoping for a family trip out. Maybe to the zoo; I love the elephants. The baby is crying again. Why? She seems really upset. Her teddy is on the floor – her mum hasn't noticed. Should I tell her?

Arthur is quiet while he does all this thinking. Mum and Kathryn have no idea how busy his mind is – to them, he's just in his own little world. Eventually, Arthur will decide whether to mention the teddy on the floor. *Eventually* – he's going to take a little time to think about that first. He's not a slow boy. He's not shy. He's just thinking.

As he grows up, people will say of Arthur that he's a deep, intelligent, intuitive child. They're right – and he's that way because of the heightened awareness and careful thinking that come with being highly sensitive

---

Musing Megan

At parents' evening, Megan's teacher tells her parents that her listening skills are poor. 'She's frequently distracted,' the teacher explains. 'Staring at the floor, or out of the window. Sometimes I have to call her name two, three times to get her attention, and even then she sometimes seems indifferent. When I can get her to focus on me, it's clear she hasn't a clue what she's meant to be doing.'

Megan isn't a bad student. She's simply distracted. Instead of listening to her teacher, she's busy thinking about something else – an upsetting argument she had with a friends at playtime, perhaps. She doesn't mean to drift off; she can't help the need to think.

Chapter 3: Experiencing Intensely

A highly sensitive child experiences the world in a different way to a non-highly sensitive child. It's brighter. It's bigger. It's bolder. It's louder. It's scarier. Same world, different experiences of living in it.

Think, for a moment, of life as a film. For a non-highly sensitive child, life is a film on the television set – colourful and noisy but not intensely so. For a sensitive child, life is a film on a cinema screen. In vibrant Technicolour. In 3D with jump-out-at-you graphics. In High Definition with astonishingly sharp details. In Dolby Surround Sound turned up so loud you can physically *feel* the soundtrack thrumming through your body. The non-highly sensitive child finds it quite easy to detach from the film. The highly sensitive child is gripped by its intensity.

Juggling lots of feelings at once

In Chapter 2 I set a scene of Kathryn, Arthur and Mum in a cafe. The children notice details of their surroundings, and think about these details, to differing degrees. But beyond noticing and considering, how do they *feel* in the cafe?

Kathryn is having a good time. She likes the smell of the coffee and the taste of her milkshake, and her blueberry muffin is pretty good. The chair she's sitting on is a bit hard, but not so much it really bothers her. She's enjoying chatting to Mum, and to her the busyness and noise around is a pleasing buzz.

Arthur is torn – he's having a good time and he's having a bad time all at once. His blueberry muffin is DELICIOUS, the best cake he's ever tasted. And the milkshake is really, really good; amazingly good! Plus it's lovely and warm in here: not too hot, not too cold, just right for Arthur. But it's so loud – his head is spinning! And so crowded – he feels hemmed in! And the sweaty smell nearby is horrid! And his seat is horrendously hard and getting itchier by the minute! And to top it all off, there's talk of a soft-play party – Arthur hates all the noise there. And Mum looks tired, which really worries Arthur – she was up with him twice last night with his bad dreams; is it his fault?

Kathryn is pretty calm inside, but Arthur is contending with a lot of feelings at once. This is typical for highly sensitive child – they're sensitive in many ways, so they feel many things.

Dialling all emotions up

Back to the cafe – how intense are the children's feelings?

- Kathryn *likes* what she smells and tastes. Her muffin is *pretty good*. She's *not bothered* really by her chair. The buzz is *pleasing*.

- Arthur's snack is *DELICIOUS, amazingly good*. It's *lovely* and warm for him. But *so* loud and *so* crowded. The smell is *horrid*. The seat is *horrendously* hard. And Arthur *hates* the soft-play idea, and he's *really worried* he's made Mum tired.

Not only does Arthur have more feelings inside right now than Kathryn, but they're deeper ones – ones that really affect him.

Feeling the intensity for longer

In the cafe, the two children feel quite different. But what if I put them in a situation in which they both feel the same way? How easily does each child bounce back from their feeling?

Mum, Kathryn and Arthur leave the cafe and head down the street. A white-haired man is walking slowly towards them. He catches his foot on a loose paving stone and falls to the ground with a cry. Mum, Kathryn and Arthur rush over to the man,

who is struggling to get up. *'I'm okay,'* he says. *'Ju
hand, will you?'* Mum takes his arm and helps hi
'Are you sure you're all right?' she asks. *'Fit as a fid\
the man, and he smiles at them all, pats Mum on the ヽ╷╷oulder
and heads off down the street.

During this little drama, Kathryn felt worried for the man and
upset that he may be hurt. As the man walks off, her anxiety
dissolves and she goes back to happily thinking about her
birthday party.

Arthur, meanwhile, was deeply distressed by the man's
accident. In fact, he burst into tears. As the man walks off,
Arthur is unable to stop crying. He still fears the fear, the
horror, the acute anxiety that came upon him in the moment
the man fell.

The man is fine, and Kathryn is fine, but Arthur is not. It will take
some time before he feels calm again. His feelings are so intense, it
takes longer to work through them and let them go.

Riding the highs and lows

The nature of intensity means life is something of a rollercoaster, up
and down, up and down (and sometimes – which can be hard to
fathom – up *and* down all at once).

The highly sensitive child experiences amazing highs. The sun is
shining, the sky is blue, the birds are singing... life is just wonderful!

The highly sensitive child also experiences challenging lows. The
clouds are thick, the rain is plummeting, the cute little baby bird that
once sang sweetly is lying dead in the garden, half-eaten by a bird...
life is immensely painful.

With practice, the wonder of the highs comes to outweigh the
horror of the lows. But to be a highly sensitive child is to be forever

riding a rollercoaster. And as the next chapter explains, that's a pretty exhausting way to live.

Passionate Penelope

Penelope reads the first Harry Potter book. Oh, she loves it! For the next fortnight, she spends all her free time ploughing through books two to seven. Amazing! A week later she's watched all the movies and spent many hours on the Pottermore website and made a birthday list on which every item is Harry Potter merchandise and badgered her parents incessantly to take her on the Harry Potter studio tour. Penelope's love for the Harry Potter is so intense, there's little room for anything else. She's Potter-mad. Until, one day, she sees a trailer for the new Batman movie...

Chapter 4: Overloading

Arthur is in the supermarket with their mum. In the time it takes Mum to select a bunch of bananas and put them into the trolley, Arthur has noticed:

> *The seat of the trolley is hard and cold. The fluorescent lights above are bright and one is making a buzzing sound like a bee. There's something sticky and a bit yucky on the handle of the trolley. The label inside his t-shirt is itching. Mum is wearing her purple skirt again. That man over there has a red beard. The air tastes like the seaside on a hot day. That lady choosing strawberries is humming a tune. The apples are very, very green. There's a fishy stink in the air. There are many bananas and some are in bunches but some are single, and some are all yellow but some have brown spots, and some are small and some are big, and some are curvy and some are quite straight...*

It all sounds rather exhausting, doesn't it? Well, that's just a snapshot of life for a highly sensitive child – and it doesn't even include the many deep thoughts and feelings that Arthur has in this timeframe. Is it any wonder that sometimes it all becomes too much for Arthur?

The Goldilocks effect: It's all too...

Do you remember the fairy story of Goldilocks and the Three Bears? Well, Goldilocks was, I suspect, a highly sensitive child (albeit it a naughty one!). The bears' chairs were too hard, and then too soft, and then just right. The porridge was too hot, and then too cold, and then just right. The beds were too high, and then too low, and then just right.

The keyword here is *too*. So much feels 'too…' to a highly sensitive child. Too salty, too sweet, too coarse, too slimy, too loud, too enclosed.

The highly sensitive child doesn't do well with 'too'. While they can tolerate a certain amount of 'too' in life (they have to in order to function), sometimes a 'too' comes along that pushes them too far.

Becoming overstimulated

All children need stimulation. All parents come to recognise that there's a fine line between just enough stimulation and too much. 'Just enough' means children are engaged, interested and focused. 'Too much' means children are overstimulated, which typically means that they:

- Act 'wired' or 'hyper' – boisterous, silly, loud

- Are distracted – they're up in the clouds

- Struggle to calm down – even when grownups get cross

Both Kathryn and Arthur get overstimulated.

- Kathryn gets overstimulated occasionally. It happens at children's birthday parties (especially her own), and the family's annual outing to a theme park leaves her pinging off the walls at bedtime. Since the situations that overstimulate Kathryn are pretty rare, it's not an issue – Mum and Dad simply ride it out.

- Arthur gets overstimulated quite often. He gets overstimulated at children's birthday parties (especially his own), and the family's annual outing to a theme park leaves him pinging off the walls at bedtime. But he can also get overstimulated on a shopping trip, at preschool, in the park, even during some full-on playing at home.

Arthur's threshold for becoming overstimulated is lower than Kathryn's, because he's more sensitive to stimuli.

Intense India

India's family have moved house, and their new neighbours have invited them over for a barbeque. India doesn't want to go – strange people, strange house, strange garden, and she's sure the food will be strange too.

But Mum and Dad insist: she's going.

Four hours later, India doesn't want to leave the barbeque. Really, really doesn't want to leave. She's having the best time ever! The kids next door are brilliant! Their toys are great! She's got room for at least five more hotdogs!

But Mum and Dad insist: she's going.

India tells her parents she hates them, then stomps all the way home and shuts herself in her room for a monster crying session.

Feeling overwhelmed

Overstimulation, a head full of thoughts, a heart bursting with feeling – all these can become overwhelming. Highly sensitive adults frequently feel overwhelmed, and they are much more experienced, knowledgeable and mature than children. Imagine, then, how easily a highly sensitive child can feel that the big, daunting, exhausting world is too much.

Add to that the highly sensitive child's lack of understanding of their own reaction:

Arthur is at his sister's birthday party. Coaxed in there by his excited sister, he's in the ball pool of the soft play. All around

21

him a sea of colourful, squishy foam balls heaves and surges, set in motion by twenty jostling, jumping children. Above the sound of their shouts and squeals, music is pounding.

Tears are pricking at Arthur's eyes. He doesn't want to cry. He doesn't want to ruin the party, or get laughed at by the other children, or get told off for creating a drama. He's fighting the tears, and they're quickly turning to anger.

Arthur doesn't know why he's tearful, and he doesn't know why his heart is beginning to pound and he's about ready to pick up some balls and hurl them across the room in rage. He watches the other children playing happily, and he wonders what's wrong with him.

An adult can see at a glance that Arthur is simply overwhelmed by his environment. But Arthur is only little. Without support from a grownup, he isn't able to understand what he's feeling, much less why, and even less what he can do to feel better.

Way too much, a little too much

Full-scale overload is about a specific situation – like Arthur at the party. It's fairly easy to spot:

- **The child shows signs of overload.** They cry, they have a tantrum, they're hyperactive, they're withdrawn, they complain of stomach ache.

- **The parents feels a touch overloaded too.** Sensitive parents are likely having a similar experience to the highly sensitive child, though hopefully coping better. But even a non-highly sensitive parent can recognise that a situation is quite full-on. Really, how many parents love the clamour and chaos of a soft-play party?

But life isn't always way too much for the highly sensitive child. It's often just a little too much. *Often.* The highly sensitive child may feel bothered by all sorts of things on a day-to-day basis: an itchy label in a pyjamas worn each night; a broken smoke alarm that beeps softly but incessantly for weeks; a funny smell coming from the bath plug hole. How big a bother is, and how many little bothers add up to one big one, depends on how sensitive the child is.

Arthur's dad cooks them dinner: baked potato with cheese. When Arthur sees the plate, he says at once, 'No! They can't be touching! The potato goes there, and the cheese goes there, not together! That's how Mum makes it!' Arthur's father says, 'Don't be silly. It makes no difference. Be grateful for your dinner and eat it.' Arthur bursts into tears. Dad gets angry.

Dad can't understand why Arthur is in such a state over a baked potato with cheese. It doesn't remotely bother him to have the cheese on top of his potato, melting nicely. He thinks Arthur is being very fussy, and making a mountain out of a molehill.

Arthur is distraught. He really, really loves baked potato with cheese. WITH cheese. Not baked potato AND cheese all melted together. He doesn't want to make Dad cross, but he can't eat the potato and cheese this way. This is the last straw. First Dad insisted that he sit on the wrong side of the table next to the fish tank that makes that annoying dripping sound. Then Kathryn said that when he started school no one would want to play with him. Then she poked him, and it really, really hurt. Then he sipped his drink and it tasted like washing-up liquid. And now his dinner looks yucky. Arthur is really, really upset.

All Dad sees is a little boy who's being needlessly fussy about potato melded with cheese. But lots of 'a little too much' has brought Arthur to a place where he's struggling to cope.

Chapter 5: Needing So Very Much

The highly sensitive child is an intense child, and included in that intensity is an array of needs. How deeply the highly sensitive child *needs*! They need so very much. Crying. Raging. Withdrawing. Demanding. Fussing. Worrying. Complaining. All the challenges that a highly sensitive child can throw at their parents are coming from their needs.

Victim Vicky

Vicky used to be a happy at school. She had made a couple of friends who were like her – quiet, kind and thoughtful – and she would skip to school, eager to see them. Then, one day, a bigger girl in the playground teased Vicky, saying she smelled. Vicky was distraught and promptly burst into tears. Delighted by the reaction, her bully clocked her as an easy target, and the next day as she ran past her at playtime she yelled, 'Vile Vicky! Vile Vicky!' Vicky was deeply ashamed. Her friends tried to reassure her that she didn't smell and she wasn't vile, but Vicky wondered – was the bigger girl right? Was that what everyone thought of her?

Needing to feel self-worth

The highly sensitive child doesn't take criticism of any kind well. Their skin is not thick; it's paper-thin. They take cruelty extremely badly; they don't cope well with an authoritative or angry approach to telling off; they can misconstrue even positive words as being negative. This sensitivity to what other's think can lead to deep-seated feelings of shame, and play out as withdrawal, acting out or being overly keen to please others.

All the highly sensitive child wants is to feel okay in themselves – that they're doing okay, that they're not a bad person, that their way of being is just fine. With support, they can gain confidence and a sense of self-worth, but alone they be plagued by feelings of inadequacy – miserable for anyone.

Needing to feel calm

Chapter 4 explains how easily overwhelmed a highly sensitive child can be. What exactly does it mean to be overwhelmed? The verb 'to overwhelm' means:

- Bury or drown beneath a huge mass
- Give too much of something to
- Have a strong emotional effect on
- Defeat entirely
- Overpower

That's how an overwhelmed highly sensitive child feels. Overpowered. Defeated. Drowning. No one likes to feel that way. No one can handle feeling that way for long. So the highly sensitive child's most fundamental need is to feel calm. *Not* overwhelmed.

Arthur is overwhelmed at the soft-play party. He needs very badly to feel better. So he's got to do something to ease the intensity of his feelings. He may:

- Sink beneath the balls and hide.
- Put his hands over his ears and hum.
- Freeze like a statue.

Or he may do none of these things. Often, it takes an adult to recognise that a child is struggling and intervene to calm them down. Perhaps Arthur just plays on and on and on, unnoticed, and is a very emotional child come the end of the party. Or perhaps Mum takes him aside and gives him some time out.

Each highly sensitive child has their own way of calming down. Ideally, that involves being away from the source of the overload in a safe, calm, quiet space. They may prefer to be alone, or they may be happy to be with their family – but they probably don't want to be around lots of people. A calming activity can really help, something like looking at a book or drawing or water play or building with Lego, or even tidying up.

Needing to be cautious

For a long time it was assumed that a highly sensitive child was shy, or socially awkward, or anxious, or inhibited. In fact, a highly sensitive child can be outwardly confident, socially adept and extraverted. But the reason for the confusion is that highly sensitive child can sometimes stand apart when other children are diving in.

Mum takes Arthur and Kathryn to the playground. The moment they arrive they spot a brand new piece of play equipment: a wooden fort with a shiny silver slide leading out from its highest tower.

Kathryn loves climbing and she races into the play fort. Half a minute later, she appears at the top of the slide, and joyously slithers down it.

Arthur watches his sister slide down. He's still standing beside Mum. He's been taking a little time to take in this new fort, and to think about climbing up it. He loves slides. He really loves slides! And a new one is very exciting. But the tower is quite tall, and that bears thinking about.

By the time Kathryn is at the top of the slide again, Arthur has made his mind up. He climbs up into the fort and makes his way to the top tower. He sits at the top of the slide, pushes off and sliiiiiiiiiiiiiiides down to the bottom. Brilliant! He's up at once and clambering back into the fort for another go.

Both children end up having a great time in the play fort. Arthur was just a little more cautious at first, because he knew that the tall tower was potentially dangerous, and he needed to be sure in himself that it was safe to proceed.

What if Arthur had decided that the tower was just too tall? Well, then he'd have decided to give the play fort a wide berth. Perhaps he'd have stuck to the swings today instead. Then other children, and perhaps his mum, may have assumed Arthur was shy. Or cowardly.

Arthur isn't cowardly. He's cautious. And who's to say that's wrong? After all, which child is most likely to have an accident at the playground: 'Dive In' Kathryn or 'Be Cautious' Arthur?

Flying-High Freddie

When Freddie was three years old, he was a tentative soul. He loved adventures – *loved* them! – but it would take him a notable length of time to consider a situation before diving in. Ten years on, Freddie is a confident boy, and you'd never guess, based on the speed with which he launches into the fun at a theme park, that he's highly sensitive. But Freddie has been to the theme park many times before, so he's comfortable with it. And Freddie's love for the thrilling sensation of being on a ride far outweighs his old hesitancy. He adores rides; they make him feel so, so good. For many hours after riding a rollercoaster, he's still on a high. He's so high he won't sleep that night. He doesn't care; it's worth it!

Needing to connect

If the highly sensitive child lives in a safe, quiet, calm bubble with little stimulation and little interaction with others, they're happy, right? Perhaps at first – but not for long.

The highly sensitive child is no island: they're very much connected to the world. Because they *care*. They care deeply, so much so that their very soul aches at times with the depth of the feeling. They need to care. They can't turn it off – even if you want them to; even if *they* want to.

They care about people and animals.

They care about injustice.

They care about suffering.

They care about doing good in the world.

Their need to care is one of their core strengths. It's also one of the aspects of their personality that can wear them down. They can 'care too much'. They can struggle to let go of issues they feel passionately about.

> *Kathryn and Arthur watch the local television news. They see a story about a car crash in which a child has died. Kathryn thinks it's pretty sad, but a moment later she's returned to her colouring and wondering what's for dinner. Arthur remains very sad and anxious. He brings up the crash several times that evening – asking questions about it: Who was the child? How did the crash happen? Where has the child gone now she's dead? That night, he has a nightmare in which he's watching the crash happen. He cries out, and Mum soothes them. After she's gone back to bed, Arthur lies awake thinking about the crash. He imagines he is the child in the car. He imagines the car crashing. He imagines pain, and death. He cries himself to sleep.*

A tragedy that's befallen an unknown family feels personal to Arthur. It deeply saddens him. It frightens him. It haunts him.

He can't toughen up. He can't stop being so sensitive. Arthur can't help being so affected. He can't help caring – it's who he is. All Arthur can do is work through his feelings and hope he won't stumble on another terrible news story anytime soon.

Caring Callum

Callum wakes up with a sore throat. It hurts a lot, but he doesn't tell his mother – he gets dressed and goes down for breakfast and tries to pretend he's just fine. But Callum's mother notices that his voice sounds funny. She asks him whether his throat is sore. Callum wants to lie, but he's learnt from experience he can't cope with the guilt of doing that. Reluctantly, he nods. 'But I can still visit Granny in the hospital?' he tries hopefully. His mother shakes her head and explains that he can't visit the hospital if he's unwell.

Callum is distraught. Granny told him just yesterday that his visits help her get better. What if she gets worse because he wasn't there to cheer her up? But he understands that if he goes, he's risking giving Granny his sore throat. It's an impossible situation, and whatever he does, he feels he's letting down his Granny whom he loves so dearly.

Needing to create

Many highly sensitive child are highly creative in some way. That can mean being interested in the arts – music, theatre, literature, sculpture, painting, architecture and so on. And it can also mean being creative thinkers: little entrepreneurs, little trend-setters.

Creativity and sensitivity go hand in hand. The highly sensitive child who notices lots and thinks lots and feels deeply:

- **Has plenty of creative ideas:** The nature of the highly sensitive child opens them up to inspiration.

- **Finds creativity an excellent outlet:** They can work through and express thoughts and feelings through being creative.

- **Connects to certain art works:** Because they sense that their creators are just like them – highly sensitive.

Is the highly sensitive child a gifted child, then? They can be (and certainly their tendency towards perfectionism may drive them to do well). But *being* creative and *excelling* in a creative pursuit aren't the same thing. What they need isn't to be a great artist or dancer or matchstick-model-builder. They simply need to do the activity, because it fulfils them.

Needing to find meaning

Many adults try to lead meaningful lives. For the highly sensitive person, who thinks and feels deeply, meaning is especially important. Highly sensitive adults are often thinkers, dreamers, creators, entrepreneurs, game-changers, even leaders – all because meaning matters.

That ongoing journey to a meaningful life begins in childhood. So the highly sensitive child needs to:

- Ask lots of questions.

- Ask deep questions.

- Think about the answers to questions.

Sometimes, the child's questions are pretty tricky to answer: 'Why do people die?' Sometimes, their questions may make you uncomfortable: 'Why did you call in sick to work when you're not ill?' Sometimes, their questions seem a bit silly: 'Why do orange cats cross the road in summer?' But for the child, they're all Big Questions whose answers fulfil their need for meaning.

Principled Pippa

At the age of five, Pippa tells her parents that she won't eat her chicken stir-fry, because she really loves chickens. The same goes for ham sandwiches and beef-burgers: she likes pigs and cows too. Pippa's parents explain vegetarianism to her, and Pippa solemnly declares that's what she is.

'For now,' says her mother, smiling – knowing that little children are faddy.

'Forever,' says Pippa resolutely – knowing that she really, really cares for animals.

Fast-forward a decade: Pippa hasn't eaten one morsel of meat since that chicken stir-fry, and after passionate and thoughtful campaigning, she's managed to persuade her entire family to become vegetarian – on principle.

Chapter 6: Being Different

Being attuned to subtleties, living intensely, often getting overwhelmed and being driven by powerful needs: these aspects of high sensitivity add up to a single realisation:

The highly sensitive child is different.

In fact, as I mention in Chapter 1, the highly sensitive child isn't all that exceptional for their trait – they're in the company of around 20 per cent of the population. Still, it feels the odds are stacked much more significantly against them: one in a hundred, a thousand, a million. And what child, beyond a certain age, finds it easy to stand out in a crowd?

Noticing the difference

If you're reading this book, it's because you know a child who is highly sensitive (or you suspect they are). You've recognised that the child is a little different to others. Do you think the child has noticed that too? Unless the child is only a baby, I expect they do know that they have a different way of experiencing the world. After all, their high sensitivity means they notice subtleties and think about them.

So, the highly sensitive child knows they're different.

Understanding the difference

Remember Arthur at the soft-play party?

> *He doesn't know why he's tearful, and he doesn't know why his heart is beginning to pound and he's about ready to pick up some balls and hurl them across the room in rage.*

Highly sensitive children are thinkers – but they're *little* thinkers. Most adults haven't got their heads around high sensitivity, let alone children. This highly sensitive business is complicated. How can a child know why they think and feel and react in the way they do without guidance?

So, the highly sensitive child knows they're different, but they don't know why.

Judging the difference

It's a safe bet that the child has been trying to make a judgement call on their difference. We teach kids from an early age to see the world in terms of right and wrong, so they'll apply that thinking to themselves: Are they *right* to be different? Are they *wrong* to be different?

At the soft-play party, all the children except Arthur are playing happily. Arthur is aware he's not feeling and behaving like the other children. He doesn't think, *Well, I've got the right approach here – soft-play centres are hell and these other children are crazy not to see that.* He thinks, *They're happy here. Why aren't I? What's wrong with me?*

Feeling out-of-step, left out, odd, *wrong* is not uncommon for Arthur. It doesn't help that other people judge him as being wrong. How many times has he heard:

- 'You're too soft.'
- 'You're a big baby.'
- 'You're a 'fraidy cat.'
- 'You need to toughen up.'

Arthur sees his difference in negative terms. He worries that he's not normal. It doesn't occur to him that different is nothing more than different – not right, not wrong.

So, the highly sensitive child knows they're different. They don't know *why* they're different, but they know that being different is somehow a failing.

Embracing the difference

In the introduction I pose the question: What child, beyond a certain age, finds it easy to stand out in a crowd? Few, I think. All a child wants is to be accepted and loved – and being different creates anxiety that perhaps you're a little less acceptable, and so a little less loveable. Only children who get the message that they are loved and accepted as they are can embrace, rather than hate, their difference.

Mum reads The Highly Sensitive Child. Hallelujah! At last, she understands her son. She reads up on high sensitivity, and she talks to other parents of highly sensitive children. She decides that her number one mission as a mum is to teach Arthur that who he is at his core is not just absolutely fine, but in fact completely wonderful.

With patience and commitment and love and acceptance (and a good pinch of humour), over time Arthur develops good self-awareness and self-esteem. It's not always easy being highly sensitive, but he's learning about his limits and how to feel better when the world gets too much. He's more confident in being himself and making the right choices for himself – even when these set them apart from their peers.

Even better, he's found lots of positives. He's very close to Mum and Dad now – they seem to 'get' him a lot more. They've bought them a dog, and he's really enjoying caring for her. At school, he's made a best friend who likes looking at books with him and learning facts about animals. And he's developing a real passion for drawing; he won a prize in the school's arts festival! He still squabbles with Kathryn. But when, sometimes, he gets upset and she calls them a cry baby – well, he pokes his tongue out at her between the tears.

So, the highly sensitive child knows they're different, and they know why they're different. And they accept that difference, and manage that difference and, eventually, come to value and celebrate that difference.

A Final Word

Philosopher Friedrich Nietzsche wrote: *'And those who were seen dancing were thought to be crazy by those who could not hear the music.'* The highly sensitive child isn't crazy. Nor are they slow, or weak, or just 'not tough enough'. They simply dance to a tune that not everyone can hear.

I hope you have found this little book helpful in hearing the music to which the child you know dances. Once you know the tune exists, and you listen for it carefully, you'll find it's beautiful, moving, powerful music.

In this little book, I have focused on the highly sensitive child and how they experience the world, in the hope that it will help improve understanding — which is the foundation of any endeavour to help, guide, support.

You'll find more information about how you can help highly sensitive children thrive in our series of books entitled *Supporting the Highly Sensitive Child.*

63437761R00026

Made in the USA
Lexington, KY
06 May 2017